A Rumor of Soul:
The Poetry of
W.B. Yeats

Donna ~
May this introduction
+ the poems of Yeats
inspire your pilgrimage.

Jeremiah Webster

Wiseblood Books

Bismarck, ND

Copyright © 2015 by Wiseblood Books
Wiseblood Books
www.wisebloodbooks.com

Cover photograph by Jonathan Kirkpatrick, used by permission

Printed in the United States of America
Set in Arabic Typesetting

Library of Congress Cataloging-in-Publication Data
Yeats, W.B., 1865-1939
A Rumor of Soul: The Poetry of W.B. Yeats / W.B. Yeats;
1. Yeats, W.B., 1865-1939—poetry,
2. Modernism 3. Religion and Literature
4. Philosophy and Poetry
5. Jeremiah Webster

ISBN-13: 978-0692500316
ISBN-10: 0692500316

TABLE OF CONTENTS

Acknowledgments:

Special thanks to the community of Northwest University for making this project a reality: to the administration for providing a course release during the Spring 2015 semester, to my esteemed colleagues in the English Department, the first-class librarians of the Hurst Library, and to the following students who provided research and editorial assistance: Donald Kimball, Haley Moutier, and Marlene Pierce. This introduction is dedicated to my children. To Liam and Madelyn: two great lights who confirm the reality of the soul. May you ever cultivate the landscape of your mind, heart, and imagination.

"There is a light that never goes out."
The Smiths

"She didn't have a soul, nothing I could hold."
Weezer

A Rumor of Soul: The Poetry of W.B. Yeats

" ... no man can create, as did Shakespeare, Homer, Sophocles, who does not believe, with all his blood and nerve, that man's soul is immortal."[1]

W.B. Yeats

The Twenty-First Century provides little accommodation for such an epigraph. W.B. Yeats' claim is too selective, too assured in its sense of history, and guided by anachronistic suppositions. If Postmodern thought is governed by an "incredulity towards metanarratives,"[2] Yeats' statement is the antithesis. Though contemporary writers might speak of *spirit* and *soul* as conceptions of a *better you*, this is a far cry from the true self that returns, " ... to one's inviolate and eternal reality ... to live in God,"[3] the Apostle Paul's conviction that, "If there is a physical body, there is also a spiritual body,"[4] or Aristotle's definition of the soul in *De Anima* as, "the essential whatness,"[5] the, " ... cause or source of the living body."[6] The reality of the soul (if not rejected outright) has been relegated to unfashionable philosophy, New Age speculation, self-help psychology, and the funereal platitudes of well meaning relatives. As neurophilosopher Patricia Churchland argues, "The concept of the soul, though having a long and respectable history, now looks outmuscled and

13

outsmarted by neuroscience ... "[7] and that, " ... my brain, not a soul, holds the key to what makes me the way I am."[8] In such environs, the soul is a waning construct, a fairytale coping mechanism. Psychology may reign, but Psyche is bound.

And yet, belief in the soul and immortality has been the impetus of art and philosophy for centuries. Yeats' affirmation of the soul is nothing new. ψυχή [soul] is endorsed by Homer[9] and Plato.[10] "I shall dwell in the house of the Lord forever,"[11] the Psalmist declares. Anchises speaks of the soul's transmigration in *The Aeneid*,[12] Solomon declares, " ... God created us for incorruption, and made us in the image of his own eternity,"[13] and in his poem, "Second Space," the modern poet Czesław Miłosz advances the argument when he asks, "Without unearthly meadows how to meet salvation? / And where will the damned find suitable quarters?"[14] While the cultures of western antiquity disagree on the particulars of the hereafter (Inkidu speaks of a House of Dust, Jacob affirms Sheol, Achilles laments Hades, and Hercules inhabits Elysium) they uniformly believe in an afterlife. The Epicureans and Sadducees are a notable *minority* in this regard.[15] Whatever judgments might be leveled against these perspectives, such investigations into the nature of humanity and the divine are (at best) descriptive rather than prescriptive, acts of investigation rather than absolutism. Mythology and religious conviction are united in this: the soul is an intrinsic feature of human nature, independent of opinion or consensus, without which the motive for virtue is invariably lost. This virtue is not a human invention, but rather a sincere attempt to inhabit the *things of God* as revealed through history, reason, natural law, and revelation. To cite Wordsworth: "The anchor of my purest thoughts, the nurse, / The guide, the guardian of my heart, and soul / Of all my moral being."[16] It is this reality and assurance that allows Phedus to relay Socrates' death as he does:

I remember the strange feeling which came over me at being with him. For I could hardly believe that I was present at the death of a friend, and therefore I did not pity him, Echecrates; his mien and his language were so noble and fearless in the hour of death that to me he appeared blessed. I thought that in going to the other world he could not be without a divine call, and that he would be happy, if any man ever was, when he arrived there, and therefore I did not pity him as might seem natural at such a time. But neither could I feel the pleasure which I usually felt in philosophical discourse (for philosophy was the theme of which we spoke). I was pleased, and I was also pained, because I knew that he was soon to die, and this strange mixture of feeling was shared by us all; we were laughing and weeping by turns...[17]

Pepetua, an early Christian martyr, exhibits a similar belief in the eternal. Her faith is perhaps more remarkable than Socrates' in that, countenancing torture, she declares, "Stand fast in the faith, and love one another, all of you, and be not offended at my sufferings."[18] She is emboldened by Jesus' words, "I am the resurrection and the life. Those who believe in me, even though they die, will live."[19] It is belief in the soul that gives rise to one of the greatest sonnets ever written in the English language:

Death be not proud, though some have called thee
Mighty and dreadfull, for, thou art not so,
For, those, whom thou think'st, thou dost overthrow,
Die not, poore death, nor yet canst thou kill me.
From rest and sleepe, which but thy pictures bee,

Much pleasure, then from thee, much more must flow,
And soonest our best men with thee doe goe,
Rest of their bones, and soules deliverie.

Thou art slave to Fate, Chance, kings, and desperate men,
And dost with poyson, warre, and sicknesse dwell,
And poppie, or charmes can make us sleepe as well,
And better then thy stroake; why swell'st thou then;
One short sleepe past, wee wake eternally,
And death shall be no more; death, thou shalt die.[20]

These examples suggest that virtue and art derive from a belief in the incorporeal, and it is curious that even the aims of the humanist rely on a future tense, a future "life," with the betterment of society, the quality of life for our children, or an individual's legacy providing rationale for right conduct.[21] Such convictions foster courage in the face of death, fortitude in the midst of adversity, and love in the presence of hate. It should not surprise us that such qualities often arrive only at the moment of death, for what better way to endure Hamlet's "quintessence of dust"[22] than to affirm "wee wake eternally."

* * *

Literary modernism is perhaps the last residence of a classical conception of the soul. Despite the break from history and a broad disenchantment with tradition, the poets and philosophers of the early Twentieth Century, W.B. Yeats included, entertain the same questions one finds in Plato's *Timaeus* or Augustine's *Confessions*:[23] namely, a sustained inquiry into the nature of God, humanity, and the cosmos. The Moderns may have willfully constructed a cenotaph to the age of faith and reason,[24] but they were no less fervent than their forerunners. Rainer Maria Rilke's *The Book of Hours* (1905), Ezra Pound's *The Cantos* (1915-1962), Wallace Stevens' *The Man With the Blue Guitar* (1937), and T.S. Eliot's *Four Quartets* (1945) are stylistically innovative, but their themes incorporate those of Antiquity and the Middle Ages. The pantheon still plays, with Agamemnon and Leda,[25] Ulysses and Circe,[26] Dante and Hamlet[27] in attendance. For all of their efforts to "Make it New,"[28] Modern poets never escape the influence of Greco-Roman myth or Judeo-Christian revelation, even as they make great strides to document and/or dismember this tradition. W.B. Yeats, arguably the greatest poet of the Twentieth Century, is no exception.

Yeats understands what happens when a "deep heart's core"[29] is omitted from the appraisal of human nature. When a civilization denies this invisible angel, a debasement[30] of culture and the physical body consistently follows. Human life is reduced to behavioral instinct, naturalistic cause and effect, and when the distractions of carnival do not suffice, the gravitational pull of despair takes hold. Many of Yeats' poems are meditations on the incorporeal, unseen but apprehended, and it is difficult to imagine his poems apart from a conviction that the soul is the wellspring of a shared humanity. Consider the role of empathy in "The Wild Swans at Coole" (1919):

> The trees are in their autumn beauty,
> The woodland paths are dry,
> Under the October twilight the water
> Mirrors a still sky;
> Upon the brimming water among the stones
> Are nine-and-fifty swans.

The nineteenth autumn has come upon me
Since I first made my count;
I saw, before I had well finished,
All suddenly mount
And scatter wheeling in great broken ring
Upon their clamorous wings.

I have looked upon those brilliant creatures,
And now my heart is sore.
All's changed since I, hearing at twilight,
The first time on this shore,
The bell-beat of their wings above my head,
Trod with a lighter tread.

Unwearied still, lover by lover,
They paddle in the cold
Companionable streams or climb the air;
Their hearts have not grown old;
Passion or conquest, wander where they will,
Attend upon them still.
But now they drift on the still water,
Mysterious, beautiful;
Among what rushes will they build,
By what lake's edge or pool
Delight men's eyes when I awake some day
To find they have flown away?

The speaker "sees" the stranger apart from the known world of experience. The poem's ability to ruminate on "men's eyes" (ln. 29) that delight in the very swans that have "flown away" (ln. 30), casts imagination as the vehicle of empathy, our point of access into other people's lives. It also suggests a compelling interplay between imagination and the soul. That we are capable of imagining a reality outside of our intellectual and emotional experience ("Among what rushes will they build" [ln. 27]) raises serious questions about the true source of knowledge and understanding. Yeats' verse grafts imagination with empathy, and the heart with the existence of a soul. The poetry affirms Blaise Pascal's assertion that, "The heart has its reasons of which reason knows nothing ... "[31] and John Muir's declaration in "My First Summer in the Sierra:"

> When we try to pick out anything by itself we find that it is bound fast by a thousand invisible cords that cannot be broken, to everything in the universe.[32]

The mystery of how we perceive reality, and the manner in which virtue is fostered, makes the poetry of W.B Yeats essential reading for anyone disenchanted with modern technology and the digital promise of connection and belonging. "The Wild Swans at Coole" apprehends a timeless quality in a time-bound world. The swans' "hearts have not grown old" (ln. 22). The "unwearied state," the "soul" of these swans, is of course a projection made by the speaker, but it is right to ask where notions of eternity and the soul are derived. Is it too much to expect to find the same qualities in ourselves that we find in nature? In a flock of "nine-and-fifty swans" (ln. 6)? In a God whose "beauty is past change?"[33] For Yeats, the crisis of modernity is a slow diminishment of this kind of inquiry and discovery. This drives Yeats to embrace any discipline that explores the sublime, however unconventional it may be. In this sense, Yeats advances the sentiment made a century earlier by Walt Whitman:

When I heard the learn'd astronomer,

When the proofs, the figures, were ranged in columns before me,

When I was shown the charts and diagrams, to add, divide, and measure them,

When I sitting heard the astronomer where he lectured with much applause in the lecture-room,

How soon unaccountable I became tired and sick,

Till rising and gliding out I wander'd off by myself,

In the mystical moist night-air, and from time to time,

Look'd up in perfect silence at the stars.[34]

Despite the lucidity of Yeats' poetic endeavors, his biography is surprisingly inconsistent. For Richard Ellmann, Yeats is a "zealot in search of a creed,"[35] a man who moves from occultism, Theosophy, Irish nationalism, and Christian theology without the slightest indication that such pursuits might be incompatible. His polyglot nature finds him initiated into an order of Christian Kabbalists, entertaining the philosophy of Madame Blavatsky, believing in fairies,[36] and seeking to hybridize Christianity with Druidism. "He was committed to a search for reality — " remarks Brenda Maddox, " — in his philosophy, in his poetry and, as he saw it, in his politics,"[37] but his life seems unmoored, without fixed reference point or compass. It must be acknowledged (even in an essay as unfettered in its praise of Yeats as this one) that many of Yeats' ideas on the specific nature of the soul are deeply problematic.[38] His notion of an "Anti-Self," participation in various séances, and communication with the "daimon" Leo Africanus undermine his ruminations on the soul, and are more in keeping with the spiritualism that was fashionable during his lifetime than the circumspect philosophical tradition(s) that equally inspired his efforts.

It is Yeats' impulse toward belief in the soul that should be championed, not his methods and/or conclusions. It could be said that the poems themselves, in exploring the reality of the soul, transcend the eccentricities of their maker. Yeats' verse anticipates the status quo here in the Twenty-First Century, but with one central difference. Postmodernity insists that reality be constructed through the paradigms of class, race, sexuality, and gender, even as it paradoxically denies individual liberty and objective standards. In this post-creedal world, knowledge is a pursuit of self-actualized value rather than a search for absolute value. Our historic moment may claim modesty and tolerance in its aims, but it is consistently intolerant toward the ways of *being* and *seeing* that preceded it. One cannot imagine Yeats finding much kinship with this perspective. To read Yeats is to find oneself in the presence of a man whose vision is ever outward, wide-eyed in its curiosity, and richly historical.

* * *

It seems reasonable to suggest that the primacy of the soul is no longer a central thesis guiding Western culture. When T.S. Eliot laments the scientism of the early Twentieth Century,[39] his critique could just as well serve as a eulogy for the human soul, an element of being all but abandoned by societies that embrace the presuppositions of Marx, Engels, Nietzsche, Comte, and Durkheim. The throne of Heaven is eclipsed by the throne of

State, of Self, and any foreboding sense of an "undiscovered country"[40] is dismissed as mere hallucination. In their best moments, these are serious philosophers with legitimate critiques of socio-economic policy and religious expression. The same cannot be said of today's working philosophy. Contemporary thinkers greet such questions with a startling ambivalence, if not contempt. The irony of an Enlightenment sensibility is that the very humanism it champions consistently debases the human individual in its implementation. The result is a cultural milieu, particularly in America, where irony is the last virtue standing, what David Foster Wallace describes as " ... a sort of existential poker face ... the new junta, using the very tool that exposed its enemy to insulate itself."[41] In such a world, parody and satire become a student's introduction to Rodin, the Sistine Chapel, Shakespeare, Beethoven's Fifth, and the poems of Emily Dickinson.[42] Culture becomes a nihilism of cynical memes and hashtags, a status update from Nietzsche's Last Man,[43] a world where citizens are indeed *clever* and *nice*, but for no particular reason.

This reality is omnipresent in popular culture and the academy today. "Afterlife," Win Butler of *Arcade Fire* sings, "O my God, what an awful word."[44] In less celebrity-laden quarters, modern philosophers acknowledge the same. In *The Revenge of Conscience* (1999), J. Budziszewski describes it this way:

> By contrast with the Classical way of affirming absolute values, the Pluralist way is *anoetic* and *anapologetical*. Pluralists are anoetic because they *do* take the Babel around them at face value. Their arguments appeal to shared ignorance rather than shared knowledge .... The Pluralist denies the need to make one voice in the Babel his own; he refuses to stake out a position, then argue its

claims on their merits. By adopting a position of neutrality among competing goals and aspirations, of equal concern and respect for them all (that becomes one of his absolutes), he tries to escape the futility of interminable apologetics and carve out a new moral sphere in which people of every point of view can get along: sodomists with socialists, pickpockets with Platonists, hedonists with *Hassidim*.[45]

In *All Things Shining* (2011), professors Hubert Dreyfus and Sean Dorrance Kelly adopt this position by divorcing the pagan gods from the supernatural and reducing the soul to a "whooshing up"[46] of ineffable, albeit transitory, experiences. In a sincere attempt to combat the forces of nihilism and religious fanaticism in contemporary society, Dreyfus and Kelly find solace in " ... Greek polytheism as it is portrayed by Homer."[47] They argue that the modern sporting event is a close approximation of *kleos* [glory] as the Greeks understood it.[48] The athleticism of a perfect tennis serve, a goal in the World Cup, or a Super Bowl touchdown pass are moments where individuals construct meaning. Through a generous revision of the polytheistic worldview (Human sacrifice and patriarchy are out. Populism is in.), Dreyfus and Kelly suggest that the sacred can be evoked as *physis* and *poietic* without an objective reality. Unfortunately, in an effort to "propitiate the divine,"[49] and "lure back the gods of old"[50] Dreyfus and Kelly lose sight of both. Their vision of the sacred is entirely secular. As they state in their concluding remarks:

The practices have gathered throughout the history of the West to reveal these manifold ways the world is. Perhaps there are other ways the practices have gathered too. But only now, released from the ancient temptation to monotheism, can we find a place for each of these ways of being in our contemporary world. The polytheism that gets all these ways in balance will be more varied and more vibrant than anything Homer ever knew.

This contemporary Polytheistic world will be a wonderful world of sacred shining things.[51]

Is such a broad and arbitrary embrace of "all things shining" our only consolation as we gaze into the abyss? Must we content ourselves with the turgid gods of sport and leisure? Is the Colosseum our only sanctuary? For those who affirm the soul this brand of heterodoxy is disconcerting, for it is too often the absence of cohesion and unity, a disharmony encouraged by the trends of moral relativism and political correctness. As G.K. Chesterton observed a century earlier:

> Polytheism, therefore, was really a sort of pool; in the sense of the pagans having consented to the pooling of their pagan religions. And this point is very important in many controversies ancient and modern. It is regarded as a liberal and enlightened thing to say that the god of the stranger may be as good as our own; and doubtless the pagans thought themselves very liberal and enlightened when they agreed to add to the gods of the city or the hearth some wild and fantastic Dionysus coming down from the mountains or some shaggy and rustic Pan creeping out of the woods. But exactly what it lost by these larger ideas is the largest idea of all. It is the idea of the fatherhood that makes the whole world one.[52]

This dynamic is not limited to the secular sphere. Christian expression in the United States has also committed itself to many of the same ideals. In churches today, humility is often eclipsed by hype, piety is mere performance, and Christ is lost in the rhetoric of charlatans. It is no accident that the American Christian is nearly indistinguishable from his neighbor, or that the Protestant church, no longer the keel of social activism and beatitude, too often recedes into hollow ritual and incoherent revisionism. As the Baby Boomer generation loses ascendancy, the mega-church phenomenon, that odd coupling of consumerism and the Great Commission, is likely to follow suit. The no doubt well meaning Emergent churches are equally short-sighted, so committed are their aims to notions of "relevance" at the expense of a vibrant orthodoxy. This is, perhaps, the only silver lining for those who, like Yeats, yearn for spiritual vitality in their lifetimes. The present model is, quite simply, unsustainable.

Such realities have cheapened our sense of the soul's necessity, leaving a benediction that suggests that all is indeed, *human, all too human*.[53] With little sacred left to be found in the sanctuaries, it is no wonder the gods of sex, sport, and leisure acquire such luminosity, such liturgical commitment in our day. As Leszek Kołakowski laments, "A culture that loses its sense of *sacrum*, loses its sense entirely."[54] Reduced to the tenets of materialism, life seems incapable of sustaining an eternal vision of human nature and destiny. There is too much noise, too many reminders of Thales' thesis[55] to embrace this, the grandest of all premises. From the Enlightenment forward, art and religious aspiration have increasingly aligned themselves with this belief. As Paul Claudel observes in his acerbic critique of Nineteenth-Century poetry:

> One of the most absurd and hateful scenes commonly ... is
> that of the immortality promised not to our soul (the great

Nineteenth-Century vulgarizers deny that we have one), but to those purely material elements of which we are composed. Listen to what they say, dear reader! "It is true that what you wrongly consider to be your person will perish, but your flesh will live again eternally among the roses, your breath in the blowing of the wind, your eyes in the glowing fireflies, etc." It is as if one were to say: "Here is the Venus de Milo, which I am going to reduce to rubble. It's true that it will no longer exist as a statue, but it will continue to exist as stone and powder for the sharpening of knives." I hold that from this moment the statue has wholly and absolutely ceased to exist, as much as the rose, now turned to dung. Please spare us your insipid consolations.[56]

Claudel's appraisal could just as easily be applied to the milieu of our day. An odd coupling of scientism and moral relativity has led to a denial of the soul entirely, with the gray matter of the brain now serving as heir apparent. As Francis Crick states, "The idea that man has a disembodied soul is as unnecessary as the old idea that there was a Life Force."[57] Like Laplace, Crick has *no need for that hypothesis.*[58] The personal and cultural implications of this worldview have been catastrophic. The tension is not between the false dichotomy of "Faith" vs. "Reason" as contemporary intellectuals[59] are prone to argue, but between the far less polemical impulses of our nature, what Yeats once called "the ritual of the marriage of heaven and earth:"[60] the dynamic of body and soul, discipline and decadence, knowledge and ignorance, hope and despair. The sad irony is that an age most attuned to the precepts of Darwinian evolution is proving incapable of advancing equally meaningful innovations in art, civic duty, and culture. Salmon Rushdie is right to ask, "O Dream-

America, was civilization's quest to end in obesity and trivia ... ?"[61] Only the kind of renaissance one sees in the poetry of W.B. Yeats is capable of integrating faith and reason into a single epistemology.[62] Without this reformation, individual and communal decline is assured. In their pursuit of an immortality divorced from the soul, Claudel's Nineteenth-Century poets and bohemians, Ray Kurzweil's[63] Twenty-First Century transhumanists and futurists ignore the dominant feature of our cosmos. Namely, its finitude.

There is a brilliant scene in Woody Allen's *Annie Hall* (1977) where a Mother takes her young boy to see a doctor:

MOTHER

(To the doctor)

He's been depressed. All of a sudden,

he can't do anything.

DOCTOR

(Nodding)

Why are you depressed, Alvy?

MOTHER

(Nudging Alvy)

Tell Dr. Flicker.

(Young Alvy sits, his head down.
His mother answers for him)

It's something he read.

DOCTOR
(Puffing on his cigarette and
nodding)
Something he read, huh?

ALVY
(His head still down)
The universe is expanding.

DOCTOR
The universe is expanding?

ALVY
(Looking up at the doctor)
Well, the universe is everything, and if
it's expanding, someday it will break apart
and that would be the end of everything!

(Disgusted, his mother looks at him)

MOTHER
(shouting)
What is that your business?
(she turns back to the doctor)
He stopped doing his homework.

ALVY

What's the point?

MOTHER

(Excited, gesturing with her hands)

What has the universe got to do with it?

You're here in Brooklyn! Brooklyn is not

expanding!

DOCTOR

(Heartily, looking down at Alvy)

It won't be expanding for billions of years

yet, Alvy. And we've gotta try to enjoy

ourselves while we're here. Uh?

(He laughs)[64]

Alvy perceives the central problem with materialism. His paralysis finds ready company among the Romantics, Goethe, Albert Camus, and Edward Gorey. Even if the human race is evolving ever upward and onward through a series of progressive stages (a dubious proposition at best), the entropic principle[65] is all that awaits at journey's end. Alvy is the rare individual willing to contemplate this fact. The expansion of the universe, the inevitable death of the sun, ensures our extinction, making calls for "solidarity"[66] vain attempts to create meaning out of annihilation. In *Annie Hall*, the doctor's only prescription is hedonism. In the face of mortality, many individuals choose to *amuse themselves to death*.[67] Without a vision of the soul (regardless of how vague or unorthodox it might be) it becomes far too easy to embrace the tragic irony of the following lyrics from MGMT:

> I'm feeling rough, I'm feeling raw, I'm in the prime of my life. / Let's make some music, make some money, find some models for wives. / I'll move to Paris, shoot some heroin, and fuck with the stars. / You man the island and the cocaine and the elegant cars. / This is our decision, to live fast and die young. We've got the vision, now let's have some fun. / Yeah, it's overwhelming, but what else can we do. / Get jobs in offices, and wake up for the morning commute. / Forget about our mothers and our friends / We're fated to pretend.[68]

The Poems

In *The Birth of Tragedy* (1871), Nietzsche asserts that " ... art is the supreme task and the truly metaphysical activity of this life." [69] Yeats' poems exhibit this quality and ambition. By synthesizing tradition, myth, and liturgy within the context of the subjective self, Yeats forges a poetic voice that speaks with the immediacy of the moment and the wisdom of the ages. In its search for the sublime, the poetic voice is bound to human history and far above it. It is a poetry that genuinely seeks to " ... name and number the passions and motives of men."[70] It bears mentioning that Yeats' poetry is wholly dependent on a conception of the soul and an afterlife. Consider the quest "out of nature" (ln. 25), for "what is past, or passing, or to come" (ln. 32) in "Sailing to Byzantium" (1928):

That is no country for old men. The young
In one another's arms, birds in the trees
- Those dying generations - at their song,
The salmon-falls, the mackerel-crowded seas,
Fish, flesh, or fowl, commend all summer long
Whatever is begotten, born, and dies.
Caught in that sensual music all neglect
Monuments of unageing intellect.

An aged man is but a paltry thing,
A tattered coat upon a stick, unless
Soul clap its hands and sing, and louder sing

For every tatter in its mortal dress,
Nor is there singing school but studying
Monuments of its own magnificence;
And therefore I have sailed the seas and come
To the holy city of Byzantium.

O sages standing in God's holy fire
As in the gold mosaic of a wall,
Come from the holy fire, perne in a gyre,
And be the singing-masters of my soul.
Consume my heart away; sick with desire
And fastened to a dying animal
It knows not what it is; and gather me
Into the artifice of eternity.

Once out of nature I shall never take
My bodily form from any natural thing,
But such a form as Grecian goldsmiths make
Of hammered gold and gold enamelling
To keep a drowsy Emperor awake;
Or set upon a golden bough to sing
To lords and ladies of Byzantium
Of what is past, or passing, or to come.

With "no country for old men" (ln. 1), and a trajectory for the physical body that can only result in "a tattered coat upon a stick" (ln. 10), the speaker presents an alternative to death, a Byzantium where all share in the nobility of "lords and ladies" (ln. 31) and where the "holy fire" (ln. 17) of God burns off the dross of desire "fastened to a dying animal" (ln. 22). Like Dante, who must pass through a wall of fire before he can enter paradise,[71] Yeats casts suffering as the path of entry into "the artifice of eternity" (ln. 24).[72] In this way, Yeats inhabits the metaphysical nature of art cited by Nietzsche, and yet he rejects the dispensation of materialism and "every tatter in its mortal dress" (ln. 12) in favor of a worldview that is inclusive of a transcendent reality for the soul.

In addition to his musings on the supernatural and the nature of revelation, "Soul clap its hands and sing" (ln. 11), Yeats is also committed to the preservation of history. Yeats continues to use many of the traditional forms his contemporaries had abandoned, creating a highly formalized approach to poetry. This appears to be a reaction against the fragmentation and disharmony that featured so prominently in the early Twentieth Century. As the soul serves to unify the heart, mind, and spirit of a human individual, so Yeats' commitment to form functions as a way to synthesize his political, aesthetic, and philosophical convictions. According to Delmore Schwartz, Yeats felt " ... a fundamental incongruity between his own sense of the importance of human lives and their physical smallness in the universe."[73] Schwartz goes on to describe what Yeats found so troubling:

> The development of modern culture from Darwin and Huxley to Freud, Marx, and the author of *The Golden Bough*, merely extended, hastened, and intensified this process of removing the picture of the world which the poet took for granted as the arena of his imagination, and putting in its place another world-picture which he could not use.[74]

In response to these developments, Yeats expects apocalypse even as he refashions the myths of the classical world. Consider "Leda and the Swan" (1923):

A sudden blow: the great wings beating still
Above the staggering girl, her thighs caressed
By the dark webs, her nape caught in his bill,
He holds her helpless breast upon his breast.

How can those terrified vague fingers push
The feathered glory from her loosening thighs?
And how can body, laid in that white rush,
But feel the strange heart beating where it lies?

A shudder in the loins engenders there
The broken wall, the burning roof and tower
And Agamemnon dead.
                              Being so caught up,
So mastered by the brute blood of the air,
Did she put on his knowledge with his power
Before the indifferent beak could let her drop?

The rape of Leda by Zeus is described without any of the adornment found in Renaissance depictions: "A sudden blow: the great wings beating still / Above the staggering girl" (ln. 1-2). Yeats' treatment abandons the baroque renderings of the past. Zeus is merciless and terrible: "her thighs caressed / By the dark webs, her nape caught in his bill, / He holds her helpless breast upon his breast" (ln. 2-4). Leda is unaided and severely damaged by the encounter. "A shudder in the loins engenders there / The broken wall, the burning roof and tower / And Agamemnon dead" (ln. 9-11). Yeats' account of this brutality becomes a metaphor for his age. Modernity accuses the divine of indifference, if not malevolence: Zeus and his bird beak callously dropping Leda to the floor. This is what makes Yeats' refashioning so powerful. Readers cannot think of modernity or the divine without the rape of Leda informing their meditations. The poem foreshadows the fate of Troy and the successive tragedy of the house of Atreus, all the result of Zeus' violence. The gods assume culpability for human suffering and the sins of history are cast onto future generations.

Yeats ushers this myth into modernity. "Being so caught up / So mastered by the brute blood of the air, / Did she put on his knowledge with his power / Before the indifferent beak could let her drop?" (ln. 12-15). He captures the spirit of an age that asks: What if a person's life is spent waiting for the divine? And what if that vision, rather than being one of beauty and insight, is intolerable? Such rumination is unique to modernity, when a century of pervasive atheism lost faith in religion, and even those who kept faith found it stripped of its objectivity. It also provides a telling portrait of how Yeats views the world. His entire life is an attempt to commune with the divine in a manner not afforded to Leda.

From the bleak forecast of poems like "Leda and the Swan," Yeats retreats to the pastoral or (as is the case with the early poems) embarks into the *fantastique*. In one of his letters to Katharine Tynan, Yeats refers to "The Stolen Child" (1889) as "almost all a flight into fairyland from the real world, and a summons to that flight."[75] He goes on to express a sincere desire to " ... alter that and write a poetry of insight and knowledge."[76]

As his career advances, the poetry becomes less escapist and more attuned to a genuine metaphysic. Yeats possesses enough self-awareness to know that spirituality can easily digress into mere escapism, into what he calls the poetry of "longing and complaint."[77] When the artist's imagination is not informed by reason, by history, by revelation it truly can be, to cite Marx, "the reflection of himself in the fantastic reality of heaven."[78]

Few, if any, of Yeats' poems locate themselves in urban centers or reference the industrial automation that was commonplace during Yeats' lifetime. Such absences do not negate the presence of thoroughly modernist concerns, but Yeats' style is uniquely antique among his peers. The poems retain a Romantic lyricism, with traditional sonnet forms ("In the Seven Woods") rhyming quatrains ("In the Firelight"), ottava rima ("Sailing to Byzantium"), and stanzas built upon the couplet ("The Four Ages of Men") seamlessly integrated into Yeats' poetic vision. Consider also the elegiac quality of a poem like "The Falling of the Leaves" (1889):

> Autumn is over the long leaves that love us,
> And over the mice in the barley sheaves;
> Yellow the leaves of the rowan above us,
> And yellow the wet wild-strawberry leaves.
> The hour of the waning of love has beset us,
> And weary and worn are our sad souls now;
> Let us part, ere the season of passion forget us,
> With a kiss and a tear on thy drooping brow.

Yeats sees tradition as a way to interpret the present. In a world ravaged by the industrial revolution and the "efficiency" of mechanized warfare, there is reassurance in the literary and cultural forms of the past. Like Eliot, Yeats sees art as a container and preserver of culture, a ship to endure the present tempest.

That the majority of Yeats' poems are elegies indicates an abiding dissatisfaction with modernity, and serves as the primary catalyst for his rumination on the soul, for a reality beyond the temporal. Consider also "The Lake Isle of Innisfree" (1890), the poem that initiated his career as a serious poet, and the poem Yeats unfortunately grew to despise after decades of public readings:

> I will arise and go now, and go to Innisfree,
> And a small cabin build there, of clay and wattles made:
> Nine bean-rows will I have there, a hive for the honey-bee;
> And live alone in the bee-loud glade.
>
> And I shall have some peace there, for peace comes dropping slow,
> Dropping from the veils of the morning to where the cricket sings;
> There midnight's all a glimmer, and noon a purple glow,
> And evening full of the linnet's wings.
>
> I will arise and go now, for always night and day
> I hear lake water lapping with low sounds by the shore;
> While I stand on the roadway, or on the pavements grey,
> I hear it in the deep heart's core.

The poem resides entirely in the mind's eye of the poet. On "pavements grey" (ln. 11), the speaker's imagination confronts him with a vision of a world far beyond the dystopia of modern city life. There is no discernible audience to receive the declaration, "I will arise and go now, and go to Innisfree," no fellow pilgrim to travel with the speaker, nor is the "lake water lapping with low sounds by the shore" (ln. 10), the "Nine-bean rows" (ln. 3), "bee-loud glade" (ln. 4), or "evening full of the linnet's wings" (ln. 8) verifiable apart from the "deep heart's core" (ln. 12). The final line is the apotheosis of what it means to experience a reality beyond the material senses. It is a direct challenge to the epistemologies that govern the modern age, and suggests that knowledge is, by its very nature, paradoxical: visible and invisible, spatial and spiritual. From this vantage point, the soul, the "deep heart's core" (ln. 12), is where we are able to affirm the reality of place (real and imagined), the dignity of others, of ourselves, and endure those forces that blind us to the truth of Innisfree: an island as real as any fixed point on a map.

This mediation on the poetry of Yeats can be summarized in the tale of Polydorus. A son of Priam, Polydorus flees the sacking of Troy only to be killed by the king of Thrace who was entrusted to care for him.[79] Years later, Aeneas haphazardly tears off a green branch from a dogwood to find that the spirit of Polydorus now speaks through the black blood that issues forth. The ontology that surrounds this scene from Virgil's *Aeneid* is apt. Hospitality distinguishes individuals from everything else in the natural world. The affirmation of soul one finds in Yeats' poetry affirms human distinctiveness within the created order. It delineates human atoms from birds and bats, fish and flora, planets and protozoa. The extension of grace and communion with the neighbor, the friend, and even with the enemy, acknowledges the intrinsic value of all human life. Having been denied such hospitality, Polydorus loses his physical body, his *Imago Dei*, and is resigned to the life of a plant. When the human soul is not invited to sup, degradation follows. It is no accident that the problems explored in the myth of Polydorus — a crisis of morality, of ethics, and of basic decency — preoccupies our daily headlines. The present milieu has equated human nature with the natural world, and who is inclined to weep over the snapping of twigs, the tearing of leaves, the splitting of stones?

The Darkness Drops Again

Institutions of higher learning provide various examples of what happens when a "death of soul" occurs. The resulting commodification of education must be resisted. If universities have no higher cause than assessment, career placement, and self-actualization, they owe a written apology to debt-laden graduates. Here in the West, especially in the Humanities, institutions of higher learning have abandoned a love of knowledge for its own sake, and given themselves over to corporate and political interests. An alarming number of students (by no fault of their own) now believe universities exist to provide job security, or to advance a variety of libertine and activist causes. This has created a culture where literature is either perceived as a kind of MP3 playlist, an expression of preference — arbitrary and amendable — or an anthology in service of some Anglo-hegemonic conspiracy. Not only are Homer and Dante, Austen and Cather, and increasingly, with the rise of video game studies, literature itself, asked to justify their existence, so too are professors, with a scrutiny that reminds one of Socrates before his accusers. The advent of "trigger warnings," which provide students "explicit alerts that the material they are about to read or see in a classroom might upset them,"[80] is understandable in cases of extreme trauma and abuse, but also smacks of censorship, a "fragility of mind,"[81] and a willful shutting of eyes and ears while humming against the human drama of evil and depravity. It is representative of a society that believes itself privileged enough to choose what it will engage with and ignore. It is a form of Ingsoc[82] that makes neurosis the new normal. Such attitudes cannot evoke the wisdom of Ulysses, "I am a part of all that I have met,"[83] or the counsel of Rainer Maria Rilke, "here there is no place / that does not see you. You must change your life,"[84] and the mind strains to imagine such environs ever producing a W.B. Yeats. Such genius is cultivated and refined through a controversial reading list. A list that inspires and provokes. A list that necessarily challenges an individual's presuppositions. A list that used to be called the Western Canon.

The malaise that has befallen the modern academy is also evident in the culture at large, primarily in the manner in which notions of individual freedom and liberty are articulated. However moral the pursuit of equality may be, the enterprise has become a democracy of mere consumption: a dystopia of smartphones, caramel macchiatos, YouTube humiliations, and celebrity Twitter feeds. Technologies of transcendent potential are employed for trivial ends. The comments section that accompanies most online news articles, for example, is only distressing for those seeking genuine public dialogue. Human rights are unmoored from natural law, and entitlements betray a lack of true imagination and charity.[85] The necessity of an informed and responsible citizenry is abandoned, and a misguided "freedom from necessity"[86] governs the body politic. Alexander Solzhenitsyn is prophetic when he declares, "The defense of individual rights has reached such extremes as to make society as a whole defenseless against certain individuals. It is time, in the West, to defend not so much human rights as human obligations."[87] Under the present circumstance, decadence of body and atrophy of mind prevail. It is Plato's forecast for all democracies.[88] It is a direct consequence of naturalism and the grave as terminus. It is endemic of a civilization that has lost its soul.

W.B. Yeats' poetry is a Whitmanian *yawp* against such tidings. It challenges the baseness of materialism and the pettiness of an unexamined life. It suggests that culture, art, and the academy must return to Plato's sense of soul in order to escape the vortex of nihilism. Such a claim is often met with understandable skepticism, but this is to confuse cultural preservation, artistic ambition, moral integrity, and academic rigor with mere elitism. What remains in the absence of such pursuits is a freedom not of liberty, but of license. There must be a middle way between religious fanaticism and the impotence of *every man doing what is right in his own eyes*.[89] Ultimately, this quest is a work of humility. As Dante suggests in *The Divine Comedy*, humility is the virtue from which all others derive. It is only here that we can experience the sublime as Longinus describes it:

> A lofty passage does not convince the reason of the reader, but takes him out of himself. That which is admirable ever confounds our judgment, and eclipses that which is merely reasonable or agreeable. To believe or not is usually in our own power; but the Sublime, acting with an imperious and irresistible force, sways every reader whether he will or no. Skill in invention, lucid arrangement and disposition of facts, are appreciated not by one passage, or by two, but gradually manifest themselves in the general structure of a work; but a sublime thought, if happily timed, illumines an entire subject with the vividness of a lightning-flash, and exhibits the whole power of the orator in a moment of time.[90]

Yeats possesses this quality, this "lightning-flash" of being "out of himself" as his poems explore the range of the possible. By refashioning the myths of Antiquity and his own Irish heritage, the poems assume a prophetic intensity. It is the same voice inhabited by Tiresias and Virgil, the Anglo-Saxon scop and the anonymous bard. This is perhaps most evident in "The Second Coming" (1920):

Turning and turning in the widening gyre
The falcon cannot hear the falconer;
Things fall apart; the centre cannot hold;
Mere anarchy is loosed upon the world,
The blood-dimmed tide is loosed, and everywhere
The ceremony of innocence is drowned;
The best lack all conviction, while the worst
Are full of passionate intensity.

Surely some revelation is at hand;
Surely the Second Coming is at hand.
The Second Coming! Hardly are those words out
When a vast image out of Spiritus Mundi
Troubles my sight: somewhere in sands of the desert;
A shape with lion body and the head of a man,
A gaze blank and pitiless as the sun,
Is moving its slow thighs, while all about it
Reel shadows of the indignant desert birds.

The darkness drops again but now I know
That twenty centuries of stony sleep
Were vexed to nightmare by a rocking cradle,
And what rough beast, its hour come round at last,
Slouches towards Bethlehem to be born?

In a world where "the best lack all conviction" (ln. 7), and "the worst / Are full of passionate intensity" (ln. 7-8), the poem anticipates "some revelation" (ln. 9). This revelation may be apocalyptic, a "rough beast" (ln. 21) who "Slouches towards Bethlehem to be born" (ln. 22), but catastrophe is preferable to the lotus-like acedia and degeneracy of the age. Without a conception of the afterlife, without a belief in the soul, "The Second Coming" is all horror show, a demonstration of Nietzsche's *ressentiment*. Viewed through the lens of tradition and religious faith however, the poem is an unflinching appraisal of the "widening gyre" (ln. 1). The poem names the malady, illuminates the crisis being ignored, and like all prophetic texts, sees desolation as a place of insight and revelation. It harkens back to the Hebrew prophets, echoing the words of Ezekiel:

> The inhabited cities shall be laid waste, and the land shall become a desolation; and you shall know that I am the Lord.
>
> The word of the Lord came to me: Mortal, what is this proverb of yours about the land of Israel, which says, 'The days are prolonged, and every vision comes to nothing'? Tell them therefore, 'Thus says the Lord God: I will put an end to this proverb, and they shall use it no more as a proverb in Israel.' But say to them, The days are near, and the fulfilment of every vision. For there shall no longer be any false vision or flattering divination within the house of Israel. But I the Lord will speak the word that I speak, and it will be fulfilled. It will no longer be delayed; but in your days, O rebellious house, I will speak the word and fulfil it, says the Lord God.[91]

Yeats' willingness to employ the prophetic voice is a surprisingly common feature of Modern poetry. Like Eliot, Pound, H.D., Rilke, and Jeffers, Yeats is eager to see what new light the cadences of religion and myth might cast on contemporary life. This creates a quality in which the aspirations of the saints, of the cloud of witnesses that have gone before us, mirrors our own. In this sense, Yeats exhibits the best kind of education and life work. Yeats' poems are not only informed by the ancients, but rapturously enchanted by them as well. They evidence the soul that resides in us all, and strive for moments that, however briefly, apprehend the sublime. As Richard Ellmann observes:

... to follow him from the beginning to the end of his life is to conclude that he was one of the true heroes of literature, who fought past weakness and conventionality only with the utmost labour. His life was a continual combat, and he chose the hardest battles when he might have chosen easier ones.[92]

Postlude

The poems included in this volume enliven a reader's sense of
the possible not just in this life but in the life to come. W.B. Yeats
not only affirms the existence of the soul, but he writes as though
his readers are genuinely in possession of one. As C.S. Lewis so
eloquently affirms:

> There are no ordinary people. You have never talked to a
> mere mortal. Nations, cultures, arts, civilizations − these
> are mortal, and their life is to ours as the life of a gnat. But
> it is immortals whom we joke with, work with, marry,
> snub, and exploit − immortal horrors or everlasting
> splendors.[93]

This collection is broad enough to inhabit the landscape of
Yeats' poetic aspirations, and it is remarkable to witness how
focused the project is from *Crossways* (1889) to *The Tower*
(1928). If spiritual despondency afflicts the inhabitants of the
Twenty-First Century, the poetry of W.B. Yeats may yet provide
an avenue to restore their sense of God, of self, of education, of
romance, of art, of departed nymphs,[94] and of "soules deliverie."[95]
It seeks remedy for what George Steiner has called a "nostalgia for
the absolute."[96] A rumor of soul haunts each of these poems. It is
a rumor that strives after the very nature of God. These poems
encourage readers to remain wildly curious toward the "infinite
spaces,"[97] and deeply suspicious of any belief (secular or religious)
that might disparage the beauty of "dappled things."[98] There is
perhaps no better summation of Yeats' project than the words of
Ismael:

Methinks we have hugely mistaken this matter of Life and Death. Methinks that what they call my shadow here on earth is my true substance. Methinks that in looking at things spiritual, we are too much like oysters observing the sun through the water, and thinking that thick water the thinnest of air. Me thinks my body is but the lees of my better being.[99]

Jeremiah Webster

June 2015

Jeremiah Webster earned a PhD in English from the University of Wisconsin-Milwaukee. His poetry has appeared in various journals including *North American Review*, *Beloit Poetry Journal*, *Crab Creek Review*, *The Midwest Quarterly*, *Floating Bridge Review*, *Rock and Sling*, *Ruminate*, *Dappled Things*, *REAL*, and elsewhere. He co-edited *The Spirit of Adoption* (Cascade Books 2014), an anthology of adoption narratives, and provided a critical introduction for *Paradise in The Waste Land* (2013), also published by Wiseblood Books. He teaches literature and writing at Northwest University in Kirkland, Washington.

The Cloak, the Boat, and the Shoes

'WHAT do you make so fair and bright?'
'I make the cloak of Sorrow:
O lovely to see in all men's sight
Shall be the cloak of Sorrow,
In all men's sight.'
'What do you build with sails for flight?'
'I build a boat for Sorrow:
O swift on the seas all day and night
Saileth the rover Sorrow,
All day and night.'
What do you weave with wool so white?'
'I weave the shoes of Sorrow:
Soundless shall be the footfall light
In all men's ears of Sorrow,
Sudden and light.'

Ephemera

'YOUR eyes that once were never weary of mine
Are bowed in sorrow under pendulous lids,
Because our love is waning.'
And then She:
'Although our love is waning, let us stand
By the lone border of the lake once more,
Together in that hour of gentleness
When the poor tired child, passion, falls asleep.
How far away the stars seem, and how far
Is our first kiss, and ah, how old my heart!'
Pensive they paced along the faded leaves,
While slowly he whose hand held hers replied:
'Passion has often worn our wandering hearts.'
The woods were round them, and the yellow leaves
Fell like faint meteors in the gloom, and once
A rabbit old and lame limped down the path;
Autumn was over him: and now they stood
On the lone border of the lake once more:
Turning, he saw that she had thrust dead leaves
Gathered in silence, dewy as her eyes,
In bosom and hair.
'Ah, do not mourn,' he said,
'That we are tired, for other loves await us;
Hate on and love through unrepining hours.

Before us lies eternity; our souls
Are love, and a continual farewell.'

The Falling of the Leaves

AUTUMN is over the long leaves that love us,
And over the mice in the barley sheaves;
Yellow the leaves of the rowan above us,
And yellow the wet wild-strawberry leaves.
The hour of the waning of love has beset us,
And weary and worn are our sad souls now;
Let us patt, ere the season of passion forget us,
With a kiss and a tear on thy drooping brow.

The Meditation of the Old Fisherman

YOU waves, though you dance by my feet like children at
    play,
Though you glow and you glance, though you purr and
    you dart;
In the Junes that were warmer than these are, the waves
    were more gay,
When I was a boy with never a crack in my heart.
The herring are not in the tides as they were of old;
My sorrow! for many a creak gave the creel in the-cart
That carried the take to Sligo town to be sold,
When I was a boy with never a crack in my heart.
And ah, you proud maiden, you are not so fair when his
    oar
Is heard on the water, as they were, the proud and apart,
Who paced in the eve by the nets on the pebbly shore,
When I was a boy with never a crack in my heart.

The Ballad of the Foxhunter

'Lay me in a cushioned chair;
Carry me, ye four,
With cushions here and cushions there,
To see the world once more.

'To stable and to kennel go;
Bring what is there to bring;
Lead my Lollard to and fro,
Or gently in a ring.

'Put the chair upon the grass:
Bring Rody and his hounds,
That I may contented pass
From these earthly bounds.'

His eyelids droop, his head falls low,
His old eyes cloud with dreams;
The sun upon all things that grow
Falls in sleepy streams.

Brown Lollard treads upon the lawn,
And to the armchair goes,
And now the old man's dreams are gone,
He smooths the long brown nose.

And now moves many a pleasant tongue
Upon his wasted hands,
For leading aged hounds and young
The huntsman near him stands.

'Huntsmam Rody, blow the horn,
Make the hills reply.'
The huntsman loosens on the morn
A gay wandering cry.

Fire is in the old man's eyes,
His fingers move and sway,
And when the wandering music dies
They hear him feebly say,

'Huntsman Rody, blow the horn,
Make the hills reply.'
'I cannot blow upon my horn,
I can but weep and sigh.'

Servants round his cushioned place
Are with new sorrow wrung;
Hounds are gazing on his face,
Aged hounds and young.

One blind hound only lies apart
On the sun-smitten grass;

He holds deep commune with his heart:
The moments pass and pass:

The blind hound with a mournful din
Lifts slow his wintry head;
The servants bear the body in;
The hounds wail for the dead.

The Rose of the World

WHO dreamed that beauty passes like a dream?
For these red lips, with all their mournful pride,
Mournful that no new wonder may betide,
Troy passed away in one high funeral gleam,
And Usna's children died.
We and the labouring world are passing by:
Amid men's souls, that waver and give place
Like the pale waters in their wintry race,
Under the passing stars, foam of the sky,
Lives on this lonely face.
Bow down, archangels, in your dim abode:
Before you were, or any hearts to beat,
Weary and kind one lingered by His seat;
He made the world to be a grassy road
Before her wandering feet.

The Lake Isle of Innisfree

I WILL arise and go now, and go to Innisfree,
And a small cabin build there, of clay and wattles made:
Nine bean-rows will I have there, a hive for the honeybee,
And live alone in the bee-loud glade.
And I shall have some peace there, for peace comes
dropping slow,
Dropping from the veils of the morning to where the
cricket sings;
There midnight's all a glimmer, and noon a purple glow,
And evening full of the linnet's wings.
I will arise and go now, for always night and day
I hear lake water lapping with low sounds by the shore;
While I stand on the roadway, or on the pavements grey,
I hear it in the deep heart's core.

When you are Old

WHEN you are old and grey and full of sleep,
And nodding by the fire, take down this book,
And slowly read, and dream of the soft look
Your eyes had once, and of their shadows deep;
How many loved your moments of glad grace,
And loved your beauty with love false or true,
But one man loved the pilgrim Soul in you,
And loved the sorrows of your changing face;
And bending down beside the glowing bars,
Murmur, a little sadly, how Love fled
And paced upon the mountains overhead
And hid his face amid a crowd of stars.

A Dream of Death

I DREAMED that one had died in a strange place
Near no accustomed hand,
And they had nailed the boards above her face,
The peasants of that land,
Wondering to lay her in that solitude,
And raised above her mound
A cross they had made out of two bits of wood,
And planted cypress round;
And left her to the indifferent stars above
Until I carved these words:
She was more beautiful than thy first love,
But now lies under boards.

The Lamentation of the Old Pensioner

ALTHOUGH I shelter from the rain
Under a broken tree,
My chair was nearest to the fire
In every company
That talked of love or politics,
Ere Time transfigured me.
Though lads are making pikes again
For some conspiracy,
And crazy rascals rage their fill
At human tyranny,
My contemplations are of Time
That has transfigured me.
There's not a woman turns her face
Upon a broken tree,
And yet the beauties that I loved
Are in my memory;
I spit into the face of Time
That has transfigured me.

To Ireland in the Coming Times

Know, that I would accounted be
True brother of a company
That sang, to sweeten Ireland's wrong,
Ballad and story, rann and song;
Nor be I any less of them,
Because the red-rose-bordered hem
Of her, whose history began
Before God made the angelic clan,
Trails all about the written page.
When Time began to rant and rage
The measure of her flying feet
Made Ireland's heart begin to beat;
And Time bade all his candles flare
To light a measure here and there;
And may the thoughts of Ireland brood
Upon a measured quietude.
Nor may I less be counted one
With Davis, Mangan, Ferguson,
Because, to him who ponders well,
My rhymes more than their rhyming tell
Of things discovered in the deep,
Where only body's laid asleep.
For the elemental creatures go
About my table to and fro,

That hurry from unmeasured mind
To rant and rage in flood and wind,
Yet he who treads in measured ways
May surely barter gaze for gaze.
Man ever journeys on with them
After the red-rose-bordered hem.
Ah, faeries, dancing under the moon,
A Druid land, a Druid tune.!
While still I may, I write for you
The love I lived, the dream I knew.
From our birthday, until we die,
Is but the winking of an eye;
And we, our singing and our love,
What measurer Time has lit above,
And all benighted things that go
About my table to and fro,
Are passing on to where may be,
In truth's consuming ecstasy,
No place for love and dream at all;
For God goes by with white footfall.
I cast my heart into my rhymes,
That you, in the dim coming times,
May know how my heart went with them
After the red-rose-bordered hem.

The Everlasting Voices

O SWEET everlasting Voices, be still;
Go to the guards of the heavenly fold
And bid them wander obeying your will,
Flame under flame, till Time be no more;
Have you not heard that our hearts are old,
That you call in birds, in wind on the hill,
In shaken boughs, in tide on the shore?
O sweet everlasting Voices, be still.

The Secret Rose

FAR-OFF, most secret, and inviolate Rose,
Enfold me in my hour of hours; where those
Who sought thee in the Holy Sepulchre,
Or in the wine-vat, dwell beyond the stir
And tumult of defeated dreams; and deep
Among pale eyelids, heavy with the sleep
Men have named beauty. Thy great leaves enfold
The ancient beards, the helms of ruby and gold
Of the crowned Magi; and the king whose eyes
Saw the pierced Hands and Rood of elder rise
In Druid vapour and make the torches dim;
Till vain frenzy awoke and he died; and him
Who met Fand walking among flaming dew
By a grey shore where the wind never blew,
And lost the world and Emer for a kiss;
And him who drove the gods out of their liss,
And till a hundred moms had flowered red
Feasted, and wept the barrows of his dead;
And the proud dreaming king who flung the crown
And sorrow away, and calling bard and clown
Dwelt among wine-stained wanderers in deep woods:
And him who sold tillage, and house, and goods,
And sought through lands and islands numberless years,
Until he found, with laughter and with tears,

A woman of so shining loveliness
That men threshed corn at midnight by a tress,
A little stolen tress. I, too, await
The hour of thy great wind of love and hate.
When shall the stars be blown about the sky,
Like the sparks blown out of a smithy, and die?
Surely thine hour has come, thy great wind blows,
Far-off, most secret, and inviolate Rose?

The Travail of Passion

WHEN the flaming lute-thronged angelic door is wide;
When an immortal passion breathes in mortal clay;
Our hearts endure the scourge, the plaited thorns, the way
Crowded with bitter faces, the wounds in palm and side,
The vinegar-heavy sponge, the flowers by Kedron stream;
We will bend down and loosen our hair over you,
That it may drop faint perfume, and be heavy with dew,
Lilies of death-pale hope, roses of passionate dream.

The Lover Pleads with his Friend for Old Friends

THOUGH you are in your shining days,
Voices among the crowd
And new friends busy with your praise,
Be not unkind or proud,
But think about old friends the most:
Time's bitter flood will rise,
Your beauty perish and be lost
For all eyes but these eyes.

He Wishes His Beloved Were Dead

WERE you but lying cold and dead,
And lights were paling out of the West,
You would come hither, and bend your head,
And I would lay my head on your breast;
And you would murmur tender words,
Forgiving me, because you were dead:
Nor would you rise and hasten away,
Though you have the will of the wild birds,
But know your hair was bound and wound
About the stars and moon and sun:
O would, beloved, that you lay
Under the dock-leaves in the ground,
While lights were paling one by one.

He Wishes for the Cloths of Heaven

HAD I the heavens' embroidered cloths,
Enwrought with golden and silver light,
The blue and the dim and the dark cloths
Of night and light and the half-light,
I would spread the cloths under your feet:
But I, being poor, have only my dreams;
I have spread my dreams under your feet;
Tread softly because you tread on my dreams.

The Fiddler of Dooney

WHEN I play on my fiddle in Dooney.
Folk dance like a wave of the sea;
My cousin is priest in Kilvarnet,
My brother in Mocharabuiee.
I passed my brother and cousin:
They read in their books of prayer;
I read in my book of songs
I bought at the Sligo fair.
When we come at the end of time
To Peter sitting in state,
He will smile on the three old spirits,
But call me first through the gate;
For the good are always the merry,
Save by an evil chance,
And the merry love the fiddle,
And the merry love to dance:
And when the folk there spy me,
They will all come up to me,
With "Here is the fiddler of Dooney!"
And dance like a wave of the sea.

In Seven Woods

The First. My great-grandfather spoke to Edmund Burke
In Grattan's house.
The Second. My great-grandfather shared
A pot-house bench with Oliver Goldsmith once.
The Third. My great-grandfather's father talked of music,
Drank tar-water with the Bishop of Cloyne.
The Fourth. But mine saw Stella once.
The Fifth. Whence came our thought?
The Sixth. From four great minds that hated Whiggery.
The Fifth. Burke was a Whig.
The Sixth. Whether they knew or not,
Goldsmith and Burke, Swift and the Bishop of Cloyne
All hated Whiggery; but what is Whiggery?
A levelling, rancorous, rational sort of mind
That never looked out of the eye of a saint
Or out of drunkard's eye.
The Seventh. All's Whiggery now,
But we old men are massed against the world.
The First. American colonies, Ireland, France and India
Harried, and Burke's great melody against it.
The Second. Oliver Goldsmith sang what he had seen,
Roads full of beggars, cattle in the fields,
But never saw the trefoil stained with blood,
The avenging leaf those fields raised up against it.

The Fourth. The tomb of Swift wears it away.
The Third. A voice
Soft as the rustle of a reed from Cloyne
That gathers volume; now a thunder-clap.
The Sixth. What schooling had these four?
The Seventh. They walked the roads
Mimicking what they heard, as children mimic;
They understood that wisdom comes of beggary.

The Arrow

I THOUGHT of your beauty, and this arrow,
Made out of a wild thought, is in my marrow.
There's no man may look upon her, no man,
As when newly grown to be a woman,
Tall and noble but with face and bosom
Delicate in colour as apple blossom.
This beauty's kinder, yet for a reason
I could weep that the old is out of season.

Never Give all the Heart

NEVER give all the heart, for love
Will hardly seem worth thinking of
To passionate women if it seem
Certain, and they never dream
That it fades out from kiss to kiss;
For everything that's lovely is
But a brief, dreamy. Kind delight.
O never give the heart outright,
For they, for all smooth lips can say,
Have given their hearts up to the play.
And who could play it well enough
If deaf and dumb and blind with love?
He that made this knows all the cost,
For he gave all his heart and lost.

O Do Not Love Too Long

SWEETHEART, do not love too long:
I loved long and long,
And grew to be out of fashion
Like an old song.
All through the years of our youth
Neither could have known
Their own thought from the other's,
We were so much at one.
But O, in a minute she changed --
O do not love too long,
Or you will grow out of fashion
Like an old song.

Words

I HAD this thought a while ago,
'My darling cannot understand
What I have done, or what would do
In this blind bitter land.'
And I grew weary of the sun
Until my thoughts cleared up again,
Remembering that the best I have done
Was done to make it plain;
That every year I have cried, 'At length
My darling understands it all,
Because I have come into my strength,
And words obey my call';
That had she done so who can say
What would have shaken from the sieve?
I might have thrown poor words away
And been content to live.

No Second Troy

WHY should I blame her that she filled my days
With misery, or that she would of late
Have taught to ignorant men most violent ways,
Or hurled the little streets upon the great.
Had they but courage equal to desire?
What could have made her peaceful with a mind
That nobleness made simple as a fire,
With beauty like a tightened bow, a kind
That is not natural in an age like this,
Being high and solitary and most stern?
Why, what could she have done, being what she is?
Was there another Troy for her to burn?

Peace

AH, that Time could touch a form
That could show what Homer's age
Bred to be a hero's wage.
'Were not all her life but storm
Would not painters paint a form
Of such noble lines,' I said,
'Such a delicate high head,
All that sternness amid charm,
All that sweetness amid strength?'
Ah, but peace that comes at length,
Came when Time had touched her form.

The Fascination of What's Difficult

THE fascination of what's difficult
Has dried the sap out of my veins, and rent
Spontaneous joy and natural content
Out of my heart. There's something ails our colt
That must, as if it had not holy blood
Nor on Olympus leaped from cloud to cloud,
Shiver under the lash, strain, sweat and jolt
As though it dragged road-metal. My curse on plays
That have to be set up in fifty ways,
On the day's war with every knave and dolt,
Theatre business, management of men.
I swear before the dawn comes round again
I'll find the stable and pull out the bolt.

The Mask

'PUT off that mask of burning gold
With emerald eyes.'
'O no, my dear, you make so bold
To find if hearts be wild and wise,
And yet not cold.'
'I would but find what's there to find,
Love or deceit.'
'It was the mask engaged your mind,
And after set your heart to beat,
Not what's behind.'
'But lest you are my enemy,
I must enquire.'
'O no, my dear, let all that be;
What matter, so there is but fire
In you, in me?'

A Friend's Illness

SICKNESS brought me this
Thought, in that scale of his:
Why should I be dismayed
Though flame had burned the whole
World, as it were a coal,
Now I have seen it weighed
Against a soul?

All Things Can Tempt Me

ALL things can tempt me from this craft of verse:
One time it was a woman's face, or worse --
The seeming needs of my fool-driven land;
Now nothing but comes readier to the hand
Than this accustomed toil. When I was young,
I had not given a penny for a song
Did not the poet Sing it with such airs
That one believed he had a sword upstairs;
Yet would be now, could I but have my wish,
Colder and dumber and deafer than a fish.

Brown Penny

I WHISPERED, 'I am too young,'
And then, 'I am old enough';
Wherefore I threw a penny
To find out if I might love.
'Go and love, go and love, young man,
If the lady be young and fair.'
Ah, penny, brown penny, brown penny,
I am looped in the loops of her hair.
O love is the crooked thing,
There is nobody wise enough
To find out all that is in it,
For he would be thinking of love
Till the stars had run away
And the shadows eaten the moon.
Ah, penny, brown penny, brown penny,
One cannot begin it too soon.

To a Friend Whose Work has Come to Nothing

NOW all the truth is out,
Be secret and take defeat
From any brazen throat,
For how can you compete,
Being honour bred, with one
Who, were it proved he lies,
Were neither shamed in his own
Nor in his neighbours' eyes?
Bred to a harder thing
Than Triumph, turn away
And like a laughing string
Whereon mad fingers play
Amid a place of stone,
Be secret and exult,
Because of all things known
That is most difficult.

Paudeen

INDIGNANT at the fumbling wits, the obscure spite
Of our old paudeen in his shop, I stumbled blind
Among the stones and thorn-trees, under morning light;
Until a curlew cried and in the luminous wind
A curlew answered; and suddenly thereupon I thought
That on the lonely height where all are in God's eye,
There cannot be, confusion of our sound forgot,
A single soul that lacks a sweet crystalline cry.

When Helen Lived

WE have cried in our despair
That men desert,
For some trivial affair
Or noisy, insolent sport,
Beauty that we have won
From bitterest hours;
Yet we, had we walked within
Those topless towers
Where Helen waked with her boy,
Had given but as the rest
Of the men and women of Troy,
A word and a jest.

The Three Hermits

THREE old hermits took the air
By a cold and desolate sea,
First was muttering a prayer,
Second rummaged for a flea;
On a windy stone, the third,
Giddy with his hundredth year,
Sang unnoticed like a bird:
'Though the Door of Death is near
And what waits behind the door,
Three times in a single day
I, though upright on the shore,
Fall asleep when I should pray.'
So the first, but now the second:
'We're but given what we have earned
When all thoughts and deeds are reckoned,
So it's plain to be discerned
That the shades of holy men
Who have failed, being weak of will,
Pass the Door of Birth again,
And are plagued by crowds, until
They've the passion to escape.'
Moaned the other, 'They are thrown
Into some most fearful shape.'
But the second mocked his moan:

'They are not changed to anything,
Having loved God once, but maybe
To a poet or a king
Or a witty lovely lady.'
While he'd rummaged rags and hair,
Caught and cracked his flea, the third,
Giddy with his hundredth year,
Sang unnoticed like a bird

Running to Paradise

As I came over Windy Gap
They threw a halfpenny into my cap.
For I am running to paradise;
And all that I need do is to wish
And somebody puts his hand in the dish
To throw me a bit of salted fish:
And there the king is but as the beggar.

My brother Mourteen is worn out
With skelping his big brawling lout,
And I am running to paradise;
A poor life, do what he can,
And though he keep a dog and a gun,
A serving-maid and a serving-man:
And there the king is but as the beggar.

Poor men have grown to be rich men,
And rich men grown to be poor again,
And I am running to paradise;
And many a darling wit's grown dull
That tossed a bare heel when at school,
Now it has filled a old sock full:
And there the king is but as the beggar.

The wind is old and still at play
While I must hurry upon my way.
For I am running to paradise;
Yet never have I lit on a friend
To take my fancy like the wind
That nobody can buy or bind:
And there the king is but as the beggar.

The Hour Before Dawn

A CURSING rogue with a merry face,
A bundle of rags upon a crutch,
Stumbled upon that windy place
Called Cruachan, and it was as much
As the one sturdy leg could do
To keep him upright while he cursed.
He had counted, where long years ago
Queen Maeve's nine Maines had been nursed,
A pair of lapwings, one old sheep,
And not a house to the plain's edge,
When close to his right hand a heap
Of grey stones and a rocky ledge
Reminded him that he could make.
If he but shifted a few stones,
A shelter till the daylight broke.
But while he fumbled with the stones
They toppled over; 'Were it not
I have a lucky wooden shin
I had been hurt'; and toppling brought
Before his eyes, where stones had been,
A dark deep hollow in the rock.
He gave a gasp and thought to have fled,
Being certain it was no right rock
Because an ancient history said

Hell Mouth lay open near that place,
And yet stood still, because inside
A great lad with a beery face
Had tucked himself away beside
A ladle and a tub of beer,
And snored, no phantom by his look.
So with a laugh at his own fear
He crawled into that pleasant nook.
'Night grows uneasy near the dawn
Till even I sleep light; but who
Has tired of his own company?
What one of Maeve's nine brawling sons
Sick of his grave has wakened me?
But let him keep his grave for once
That I may find the sleep I have lost.'
What care I if you sleep or wake?
But I'll have no man call me ghost.'
Say what you please, but from daybreak
I'll sleep another century.'
And I will talk before I sleep
And drink before I talk.'
And he
Had dipped the wooden ladle deep
Into the sleeper's tub of beer
Had not the sleeper started up.
Before you have dipped it in the beer

I dragged from Goban's mountain-top
I'll have assurance that you are able
To value beer; no half-legged fool
Shall dip his nose into my ladle
Merely for stumbling on this hole
In the bad hour before the dawn.'
Why beer is only beer.'
'But say
"I'll sleep until the winter's gone,
Or maybe to Midsummer Day,"
And drink and you will sleep that length.
'I'd like to sleep till winter's gone
Or till the sun is in his strength.
This blast has chilled me to the bone.'
'I had no better plan at first.
I thought to wait for that or this;
Maybe the weather was accursed
Or I had no woman there to kiss;
So slept for half a year or so;
But year by year I found that less
Gave me such pleasure I'd forgo
Even a half-hour's nothingness,
And when at one year's end I found
I had not waked a single minute,
I chose this burrow underground.
I'll sleep away all time within it:

My sleep were now nine centuries
But for those mornings when I find
The lapwing at their foolish dies
And the sheep bleating at the wind
As when I also played the fool.'
The beggar in a rage began
Upon his hunkers in the hole,
'It's plain that you are no right man
To mock at everything I love
As if it were not worth, the doing.
I'd have a merry life enough
If a good Easter wind were blowing,
And though the winter wind is bad
I should not be too down in the mouth
For anything you did or said
If but this wind were in the south.'
'You cry aloud, O would 'twere spring
Or that the wind would shift a point,
And do not know that you would bring,
If time were suppler in the joint,
Neither the spring nor the south wind
But the hour when you shall pass away
And leave no smoking wick behind,
For all life longs for the Last Day
And there's no man but cocks his ear
To know when Michael's trumpet cries

'That flesh and bone may disappear,
And souls as if they were but sighs,
And there be nothing but God left;
But, I alone being blessed keep
Like some old rabbit to my cleft
And wait Him in a drunken sleep.'
He dipped his ladle in the tub
And drank and yawned and stretched him out,
The other shouted, 'You would rob
My life of every pleasant thought
And every comfortable thing,
And so take that and that.' Thereon
He gave him a great pummeling,
But might have pummeled at a stone
For all the sleeper knew or cared;
And after heaped up stone on stone,
And then, grown weary, prayed and cursed
And heaped up stone on stone again,
And prayed and cursed and cursed and bed
From Maeve and all that juggling plain,
Nor gave God thanks till overhead
The clouds were brightening with the dawn.

The Realists

HOPE that you may understand!
What can books of men that wive
In a dragon-guarded land,
paintings of the dolphin-drawn
Sea-nymphs in their pearly wagons
Do, but awake a hope to live
That had gone
With the dragons?

To a Child Dancing in the Wind

DANCE there upon the shore;
What need have you to care
For wind or water's roar?
And tumble out your hair
That the salt drops have wet;
Being young you have not known
The fool's triumph, nor yet
Love lost as soon as won,
Nor the best labourer dead
And all the sheaves to bind.
What need have you to dread
The monstrous crying of wind!

Two Years Later

HAS no one said those daring
Kind eyes should be more learn'd?
Or warned you how despairing
The moths are when they are burned?
I could have warned you; but you are young,
So we speak a different tongue.

O you will take whatever's offered
And dream that all the world's a friend,
Suffer as your mother suffered,
Be as broken in the end.
But I am old and you are young,
And I speak a barbarous tongue.

A Memory of Youth

THE moments passed as at a play;
I had the wisdom love brings forth;
I had my share of mother-wit,
And yet for all that I could say,
And though I had her praise for it,
A cloud blown from the cut-throat North
Suddenly hid Love's moon away.
Believing every word I said,
I praised her body and her mind
Till pride had made her eyes grow bright,
And pleasure made her cheeks grow red,
And vanity her footfall light,
Yet we, for all that praise, could find
Nothing but darkness overhead.
We sat as silent as a stone,
We knew, though she'd not said a word,
That even the best of love must die,
And had been savagely undone
Were it not that Love upon the cry
Of a most ridiculous little bird
Tore from the clouds his marvelous moon.
ALTHOUGH crowds gathered once if she but showed her
face,
And even old men's eyes grew dim, this hand alone,

Like some last courtier at a gypsy camping-place
Babbling of fallen majesty, records what's gone.
These lineaments, a heart that laughter has made sweet,
These, these remain, but I record what-s gone. A crowd
Will gather, and not know it walks the very street
Whereon a thing once walked that seemed a burning cloud

Fallen Majesty

Although crowds gathered once if she but showed her face,
And even old men's eyes grew dim, this hand alone,
Like some last courtier at a gypsy camping-place
Babbling of fallen majesty, records what's gone.

The lineaments, a heart that laughter has made sweet,
These, these remain, but I record what's gone. A crowd
Will gather, and not know it walks the very street
Whereon a thing once walked that seemed a burning cloud.

That the Night Come

SHE lived in storm and strife,
Her soul had such desire
For what proud death may bring
That it could not endure
The common good of life,
But lived as 'twere a king
That packed his marriage day
With banneret and pennon,
Trumpet and kettledrum,
And the outrageous cannon,
To bundle time away
That the night come.

The Consolation

O but there is wisdom
In what the sages said;
But stretch that body for a while
And lay down that head
Till I have told the sages
Where man is comforted.

How could passion run so deep
Had I never thought
That the crime of being born
Blackens all our lot?
But where the crime's committed
The crime can be forgot.

The Well and the Tree

'THE MAN that I praise,'
Cries out the empty well,
'Lives all his days
Where a hand on the bell
Can call the milch-cows
To the comfortable door of his house.
Who but an idiot would praise
Dry stones in a well?'

'The Man that I praise,'
Cries out the leafless tree,
'Has married and stays
By an old hearth, and he
On naught has set store
But children and dogs on the floor.
Who but an idiot would praise
A withered tree?'

The Wild Swans at Coole

THE trees are in their autumn beauty,
The woodland paths are dry,
Under the October twilight the water
Mirrors a still sky;
Upon the brimming water among the stones
Are nine-and-fifty Swans.

The nineteenth autumn has come upon me
Since I first made my count;
I saw, before I had well finished,
All suddenly mount
And scatter wheeling in great broken rings
Upon their clamorous wings.

I have looked upon those brilliant creatures,
And now my heart is sore.
All's changed since I, hearing at twilight,
The first time on this shore,
The bell-beat of their wings above my head,
Trod with a lighter tread.

Unwearied still, lover by lover,
They paddle in the cold
Companionable streams or climb the air;
Their hearts have not grown old;
Passion or conquest, wander where they will,
Attend upon them still.

But now they drift on the still water,
Mysterious, beautiful;
Among what rushes will they build,
By what lake's edge or pool
Delight men's eyes when I awake some day
To find they have flown away?

A Song

I THOUGHT no more was needed
Youth to polong
Than dumb-bell and foil
To keep the body young.

O who could have foretold
That thc heart grows old?

Though I have many words,
What woman's satisfied,
I am no longer faint
Because at her side?

O who could have foretold
That the heart grows old?

I have not lost desire
But the heart that I had;
I thought 'twould burn my body
Laid on the death-bed,

For who could have foretold
That the heart grows old?

Lines Written in Dejection

WHEN have I last looked on
The round green eyes and the long wavering bodies
Of the dark leopards of the moon?
All the wild witches, those most noble ladies,
For all their broom-sticks and their tears,
Their angry tears, are gone.
The holy centaurs of the hills are vanished;
I have nothing but the embittered sun;
Banished heroic mother moon and vanished,
And now that I have come to fifty years
I must endure the timid sun.

The Hawk

'CALL down the hawk from the air;
Let him be hooded or caged
Till the yellow eye has grown mild,
For larder and spit are bare,
The old cook enraged,
The scullion gone wild.'
'I will not be clapped in a hood,
Nor a cage, nor alight upon wrist,
Now I have learnt to be proud
Hovering over the wood
In the broken mist
Or tumbling cloud.'
'What tumbling cloud did you cleave,
Yellow-eyed hawk of the mind,
Last evening? that I, who had sat
Dumbfounded before a knave,
Should give to my friend
A pretence of wit.'

Memory

ONE had a lovely face,
And two or three had charm,
But charm and face were in vain
Because the mountain grass
Cannot but keep the form
Where the mountain hare has lain.

The People

'WHAT have I earned for all that work,' I said,
'For all that I have done at my own charge?
The daily spite of this unmannerly town,
Where who has served the most is most defamed,
The reputation of his lifetime lost
Between the night and morning. I might have lived,
And you know well how great the longing has been,
Where every day my footfall Should have lit
In the green shadow of Ferrara wall;
Or climbed among the images of the past --
The unperturbed and courtly images --
Evening and morning, the steep street of Urbino
To where the Duchess and her people talked
The stately midnight through until they stood
In their great window looking at the dawn;
I might have had no friend that could not mix
Courtesy and passion into one like those
That saw the wicks grow yellow in the dawn;
I might have used the one substantial right
My trade allows: chosen my company,
And chosen what scenery had pleased me best.
Thereon my phoenix answered in reproof,
'The drunkards, pilferers of public funds,
All the dishonest crowd I had driven away,
When my luck changed and they dared meet my face,

Crawled from obscurity, and set upon me
Those I had served and some that I had fed;
Yet never have I, now nor any time,
Complained of the people.'
All I could reply
Was: 'You, that have not lived in thought but deed,
Can have the purity of a natural force,
But I, whose virtues are the definitions
Of the analytic mind, can neither close
The eye of the mind nor keep my tongue from speech.'
And yet, because my heart leaped at her words,
I was abashed, and now they come to mind
After nine years, I sink my head abashed.

Broken Dreams

THERE is grey in your hair.
Young men no longer suddenly catch their breath
When you are passing;
But maybe some old gaffer mutters a blessing
Because it was your prayer
Recovered him upon the bed of death.
For your sole sake -- that all heart's ache have known,
And given to others all heart's ache,
From meagre girlhood's putting on
Burdensome beauty -- for your sole sake
Heaven has put away the stroke of her doom,
So great her portion in that peace you make
By merely walking in a room.
Your beauty can but leave among us
Vague memories, nothing but memories.
A young man when the old men are done talking
Will say to an old man, 'Tell me of that lady
The poet stubborn with his passion sang us
When age might well have chilled his blood.'
Vague memories, nothing but memories,
But in the grave all, all, shall be renewed.
The certainty that I shall see that lady
Leaning or standing or walking
In the first loveliness of womanhood,

And with the fervour of my youthful eyes,
Has set me muttering like a fool.

You are more beautiful than any one,
And yet your body had a flaw:
Your small hands were not beautiful,
And I am afraid that you will run
And paddle to the wrist
In that mysterious, always brimming lake
Where those What have obeyed the holy law
paddle and are perfect. Leave unchanged
The hands that I have kissed,
For old sake's sake.

The last stroke of midnight dies.
All day in the one chair
From dream to dream and rhyme to rhyme I have
ranged
In rambling talk with an image of air:
Vague memories, nothing but memories.

Presences

THIS night has been so strange that it seemed
As if the hair stood up on my head.
From going-down of the sun I have dreamed
That women laughing, or timid or wild,
In rustle of lace or silken stuff,
Climbed up my creaking stair. They had read
All I had rhymed of that monstrous thing
Returned and yet unrequited love.
They stood in the door and stood between
My great wood lectern and the fire
Till I could hear their hearts beating:
One is a harlot, and one a child
That never looked upon man with desire.
And one, it may be, a queen.

On Being Asked for a War Poem

I THINK it better that in times like these
A poet's mouth be silent, for in truth
We have no gift to set a statesman right;
He has had enough of meddling who can please
A young girl in the indolence of her youth,
Or an old man upon a winter's night.

Upon a Dying Lady

Her Courtesy

I

WITH the old kindness, the old distinguished grace,
She lies, her lovely piteous head amid dull red hair
propped upon pillows, rouge on the pallor of her face.
She would not have us sad because she is lying there,
And when she meets our gaze her eyes are laughter-lit,
Her speech a wicked tale that we may vie with her,
Matching our broken-hearted wit against her wit,
Thinking of saints and of petronius Arbiter.

Curtain Artist bring her Dolls and Drawings

II

Bring where our Beauty lies
A new modelled doll, or drawing,
With a friend's or an enemy's
Features, or maybe showing
Her features when a tress
Of dull red hair was flowing
Over some silken dress
Cut in the Turkish fashion,
Or, it may be, like a boy's.

We have given the world our passion,
We have naught for death but toys.

She turns the Dolls' Faces to the Wall
III

Because to-day is some religious festival
They had a priest say Mass, and even the Japanese,
Heel up and weight on toe, must face the wall
-- Pedant in passion, learned in old courtesies,
Vehement and witty she had seemed -- ; the Venetian lady
Who had seemed to glide to some intrigue in her red shoes,
Her domino, her panniered skirt copied from Longhi;
The meditative critic; all are on their toes,
Even our Beauty with her Turkish trousers on.
Because the priest must have like every dog his day
Or keep us all awake with baying at the moon,
We and our dolls being but the world were best away.

The End of Day
IV

She is playing like a child
And penance is the play,
Fantastical and wild
Because the end of day

Shows her that some one soon
Will come from the house, and say --
Though play is but half done --
'Come in and leave the play.'

Her Race
V

She has not grown uncivil
As narrow natures would
And called the pleasures evil
Happier days thought good;
She knows herself a woman,
No red and white of a face,
Or rank, raised from a common
Vnreckonable race;
And how should her heart fail her
Or sickness break her will
With her dead brother's valour
For an example still?

Her Courage
VI

When her soul flies to the predestined dancing-place
(I have no speech but symbol, the pagan speech I made
Amid the dreams of youth) let her come face to face,

Amid that first astonishment, with Grania's shade,
All but the terrors of the woodland flight forgot
That made her Diatmuid dear, and some old cardinal
Pacing with half-closed eyelids in a sunny spot
Who had murmured of Giorgione at his latest breath --
Aye, and Achilles, Timor, Babar, Barhaim, all
Who have lived in joy and laughed into the face of Death.

Her Friends bring her a Christmas Tree
VII

Pardon, great enemy,
Without an angry thought
We've carried in our tree,
And here and there have bought
Till all the boughs are gay,
And she may look from the bed
On pretty things that may
please a fantastic head.
Give her a little grace,
What if a laughing eye
Have looked into your face?
It is about to die.

The Second Coming

TURNING and turning in the widening gyre
The falcon cannot hear the falconer;
Things fall apart; the centre cannot hold;
Mere anarchy is loosed upon the world,
The blood-dimmed tide is loosed, and everywhere
The ceremony of innocence is drowned;
The best lack all conviction, while the worst
Are full of passionate intensity.
Surely some revelation is at hand;
Surely the Second Coming is at hand.
The Second Coming! Hardly are those words out
When a vast image out of Spiritus Mundi
Troubles my sight: somewhere in sands of the desert
A shape with lion body and the head of a man,
A gaze blank and pitiless as the sun,
Is moving its slow thighs, while all about it
Reel shadows of the indignant desert birds.
The darkness drops again; but now I know
That twenty centuries of stony sleep
Were vexed to nightmare by a rocking cradle,
And what rough beast, its hour come round at last,
Slouches towards Bethlehem to be born?

A Meditation in Time of War

FOR one throb of the artery,
While on that old grey stone I Sat
Under the old wind-broken tree,
I knew that One is animate,
Mankind inanimate fantasy'

Sailing to Byzantium

I

That is no country for old men. The young
In one another's arms, birds in the trees
---Those dying generations---at their song,
The salmon-falls, the mackerel-crowded seas,
Fish, flesh, or fowl commend all summer long
Whatever is begotten, born, and dies.
Caught in that sensual music all neglect
Monuments of unaging intellect.

II

An aged man is but a paltry thing,
A tattered coat upon a stick, unless
Soul clap its hands and sing, and louder sing
For every tatter in its mortal dress,
Nor is there singing school but studying
Monuments of its own magnificence;
And therefore I have sailed the seas and come
To the holy city of Byzantium.

III

O sages standing in God's holy fire
As in the gold mosaic of a wall,
Come from the holy fire, perne in a gyre,

And be the singing-masters of my soul.
Consume my heart away; sick with desire
And fastened to a dying animal
It knows not what it is; and gather me
Into the artifice of eternity.

IV
Once out of nature I shall never take
My bodily form from any natural thing,
But such a form as Grecian goldsmiths make
Of hammered gold and gold enameling
To keep a drowsy Emperor awake;
Or set upon a golden bough to sing
To lords and ladies of Byzantium
Of what is past, or passing, or to come.

The Wheel

THROUGH winter-time we call on spring,
And through the spring on summer call,
And when abounding hedges ring
Declare that winter's best of all;
And after that there's nothing good
Because the spring-time has not come --
Nor know that what disturbs our blood
Is but its longing for the tomb.

Leda and the Swan

A SUDDEN blow: the great wings beating still
Above the staggering girl, her thighs caressed
By the dark webs, her nape caught in his bill,
He holds her helpless breast upon his breast.
How can those terrified vague fingers push
The feathered glory from her loosening thighs?
And how can body, laid in that white rush,
But feel the strange heart beating where it lies?
A shudder in the loins engenders there
The broken wall, the burning roof and tower
And Agamemnon dead.
Being so caught up,
So mastered by the brute blood of the air,
Did she put on his knowledge with his power
Before the indifferent beak could let her drop?

The Seven Sages

The First. My great-grandfather spoke to Edmund Burke
In Grattan's house.
The Second. My great-grandfather shared
A pot-house bench with Oliver Goldsmith once.
The Third. My great-grandfather's father talked of music,
Drank tar-water with the Bishop of Cloyne.
The Fourth. But mine saw Stella once.
The Fifth. Whence came our thought?
The Sixth. From four great minds that hated Whiggery.
The Fifth. Burke was a Whig.
The Sixth. Whether they knew or not,
Goldsmith and Burke, Swift and the Bishop of Cloyne
All hated Whiggery; but what is Whiggery?
A levelling, rancorous, rational sort of mind
That never looked out of the eye of a saint
Or out of drunkard's eye.
The Seventh. All's Whiggery now,
But we old men are massed against the world.
The First. American colonies, Ireland, France and India
Harried, and Burke's great melody against it.
The Second. Oliver Goldsmith sang what he had seen,
Roads full of beggars, cattle in the fields,
But never saw the trefoil stained with blood,
The avenging leaf those fields raised up against it.

The Fourth. The tomb of Swift wears it away.
The Third. A voice
Soft as the rustle of a reed from Cloyne
That gathers volume; now a thunder-clap.
The Sixth. What schooling had these four?
The Seventh. They walked the roads
Mimicking what they heard, as children mimic;
They understood that wisdom comes of beggary.

The Choice

The intellect of man is forced to choose
Perfection of the life, or of the work,
And if it take the second must refuse
A heavenly mansion, raging in the dark.
When all that story's finished, what's the news?
In luck or out the toil has left its mark:
That old perplexity an empty purse,
Or the day's vanity, the night's remorse.

Supernatural Songs

Ribb at the Tomb of Baile and Aillinn

I
BECAUSE you have found me in the pitch-dark night
With open book you ask me what I do.
Mark and digest my tale, carry it afar
To those that never saw this tonsured head
Nor heard this voice that ninety years have cracked.
Of Baile and Aillinn you need not speak,
All know their tale, all know what leaf and twig,
What juncture of the apple and the yew,
Surmount their bones; but speak what none ha've
heard.
The miracle that gave them such a death
Transfigured to pure substance what had once
Been bone and sinew; when such bodies join
There is no touching here, nor touching there,
Nor straining joy, but whole is joined to whole;
For the intercourse of angels is a light
Where for its moment both seem lost, consumed.
Here in the pitch-dark atmosphere above
The trembling of the apple and the yew,
Here on the anniversary of their death,
The anniversary of their first embrace,

Those lovers, purified by tragedy,
Hurry into each other's arms; these eyes,
By water, herb and solitary prayer
Made aquiline, are open to that light.
Though somewhat broken by the leaves, that light
Lies in a circle on the grass; therein
I turn the pages of my holy book.

Ribb denounces Patrick

II
An abstract Greek absurdity has crazed the man --
Recall that masculine Trinity. Man, woman, child (a
daughter or a son),
That's how all natural or supernatural stories run.
Natural and supernatural with the self-same ring are
wed.
As man, as beast, as an ephemeral fly begets, Godhead
begets Godhead,
For things below are copies, the Great Smaragdine
Tablet said.
Yet all must copy copies, all increase their kind;
When the conflagration of their passion sinks, damped
by the body or the mind,
That juggling nature mounts, her coil in their em-
braces twined.

The mirror-scaled serpent is multiplicity,
But all that run in couples, on earth, in flood or air,
share God that is but three,
And could beget or bear themselves could they but
love as He.

Ribb in Ecstasy

III
What matter that you understood no word!
Doubtless I spoke or sang what I had heard
In broken sentences. My soul had found
All happiness in its own cause or ground.
Godhead on Godhead in sexual spasm begot
Godhead. Some shadow fell. My soul forgot
Those amorous cries that out of quiet come
And must the common round of day resume.

There

IV
There all the barrel-hoops are knit,
There all the serpent-tails are bit,
There all the gyres converge in one,
There all the planets drop in the Sun.

Ribb considers Christian Love insufficient

V

Why should I seek for love or study it?
It is of God and passes human wit.
I study hatred with great diligence,
For that's a passion in my own control,
A sort of besom that can clear the soul
Of everything that is not mind or sense.
Why do I hate man, woman Or event?
That is a light my jealous soul has sent.
From terror and deception freed it can
Discover impurities, can show at last
How soul may walk when all such things are past,
How soul could walk before such things began.
Then my delivered soul herself shall learn
A darker knowledge and in hatred turn
From every thought of God mankind has had.
Thought is a garment and the soul's a bride
That cannot in that trash and tinsel hide:
Hatred of God may bring the soul to God.
At stroke of midnight soul cannot endure
A bodily or mental furniture.
What can she take until her Master give!
Where can she look until He make the show!
What can she know until He bid her know!
How can she live till in her blood He live!

He and She

VI

As the moon sidles up
Must she sidle up,
As trips the scared moon
Away must she trip:
'His light had struck me blind
Dared I stop'.
She sings as the moon sings:
'I am I, am I;
The greater grows my light
The further that I fly'.
All creation shivers
With that sweet cry

What Magic Drum?

VII

He holds him from desire, all but stops his breathing
lest
primordial Motherhood forsake his limbs, the child no
longer rest,
Drinking joy as it were milk upon his breast.
Through light-obliterating garden foliage what magic
drum?

Down limb and breast or down that glimmering belly
move his mouth and sinewy tongue.
What from the forest came? What beast has licked its
young?

Whence had they come?

VIII
Eternity is passion, girl or boy
Cry at the onset of their sexual joy
'For ever and for ever'; then awake
Ignorant what Dramatis personae spake;
A passion-driven exultant man sings out
Sentences that he has never thought;
The Flagellant lashes those submissive loins
Ignorant what that dramatist enjoins,
What master made the lash. Whence had they come,
The hand and lash that beat down frigid Rome?
What sacred drama through her body heaved
When world-transforming Charlemagne was conceived?

The Four Ages of Man

IX
He with body waged a fight,
But body won; it walks upright.
Then he struggled with the heart;
Innocence and peace depart.
Then he struggled with the mind;
His proud heart he left behind.
Now his wars on God begin;
At stroke of midnight God shall win.

Conjunctions

X
If Jupiter and Saturn meet,
What a cop of mummy wheat!
The sword's a cross; thereon He died:
On breast of Mars the goddess sighed.

A Needle's Eye

XI
All the stream that's roaring by
Came out of a needle's eye;
Things unborn, things that are gone,
From needle's eye still goad it on.

Meru

XII

Civilisation is hooped together, brought
Under a mle, under the semblance of peace
By manifold illusion; but man's life is thought,
And he, despite his terror, cannot cease
Ravening through century after century,
Ravening, raging, and uprooting that he may come
Into the desolation of reality:
Egypt and Greece, good-bye, and good-bye, Rome!
Hermits upon Mount Meru or Everest,
Caverned in night under the drifted snow,
Or where that snow and winter's dreadful blast
Beat down upon their naked bodies, know
That day brings round the night, that before dawn
His glory and his monuments are gone.

Those Images

WHAT if I bade you leave
The cavern of the mind?
There's better exercise
In the sunlight and wind.

I never bade you go
To Moscow or to Rome.
Renounce that drudgery,
Call the Muses home.

Seek those images
That constitute the wild,
The lion and the virgin,
The harlot and the child

Find in middle air
An eagle on the wing,
Recognise the five
That make the Muses sing.

Endnotes

1 George Steiner: *Real Presences* (1991) pg. 228

2 Jean-François Lyotard: *The Postmodern Condition: A Report on Knowledge* (1979)

3 Thomas Merton: *New Seeds of Contemplation* (1961) pg. 38

4 1 Corinthians 15:44 (NRSV)

5 *De Anima* (II, 412b 10) Trans. J.A. Smith

6 Ibid. (II, 415b 5)

7 *Touching a Nerve: The Self as Brain* (2013) pg. 63

8 Ibid pg. 32

9 *Iliad* (I, ln. 1-5)

10 See *Phaedo* and *Charmides*

11 See "Psalm 23"

12 *The Aeneid* (VI, ln. 724-751)

13 The Wisdom of Solomon 2:23 (NRSV)

14 *Second Space* (2004) pg. 3

15 Epicurus denied the existence of an immortal soul and advocated for an ethic of reciprocity and hedonism. The Sadducees denied the resurrection of the dead.

16 "Lines Composed A Few Miles Above Tintern Abbey" (1798) ln. 109-111

17 See *Phaedo: The Trial and Death of Socrates* (1992) pg. 56 Trans. Benjamin Jowett

18 Donna Kafer: *Women of Faith* (2008) pg. 95

19 John 11:25

20 John Donne: "Holy Sonnet 10" (1633)

21 It is worth noting that these hopes and aspirations are as speculative as the afterlife encouraged by religious faith.

22 *Hamlet* (Act II, Scene ii)

23 See Book X

24 In addition, we cannot overestimate the impact of the world wars on the philosophy and psyche of the Twentieth Century.

25 W.B. Yeats: "Leda and the Swan" (1923)

26 Ezra Pound: "The Cantos" (1915-1962)

27 See Eliot's "The Love Song of J. Alfred Prufrock" (1920) and "The Waste Land" (1922)

28 Ezra Pound's famous maxim describing the aims of Modern poetry.

29 "The Lake Isle of Innisfree" (1888)

30 Idolatry is another possibility, but in both cases a distortion of priority and value occurs.

31 From *Pensées* (1670) No. 423

32 Chapter Six: *Mount Hoffman and Lake Tenaya*

33 See Hopkins' "Pied Beauty" (1877) ln. 10

34 From *Leaves of Grass* (1881-1882 edition)

35 *Yeats: The Man and the Mask* (1948) pg. 42

36 Ibid. According to Ellmann, " ... If pressed he will say he believes in them as 'dramatizations of our moods.'" pg. 116

37 *Yeats's Ghosts: The Secret Life of W.B.Yeats* (2000) pg. 225

38 See "Anima Hominis" (1924)

39 "Thoughts After Lambeth" (1930)

40 *Hamlet* (Act III, Scene i)

41 "E Unibus Pluram: Television and U.S. Fiction" (1993)

42 We can only imagine how powerful these works of art would have been in their original context.

43 From *Thus Spoke Zarathustra* (1891): "'What is love? What is creation? What is longing? What is a star?' thus asks the last man, and blinks. The earth has become small, and on it hops the last man, who makes everything small. His race is as ineradicable as the flea; the last man lives longest." (*Zarathustra's Prologue*, v)

44 "Afterlife" from the album *Reflektor* (2013)

45 Chapter One pg. 8-9

46 Chapter Seven pg. 201

47 Chapter One pg. 21

48 See Chapters Three and Seven

49 Chapter Seven pg. 198

50 Chapter Seven pg. 222

51 Ibid pg. 223

52 *The Everlasting Man* (1925), Part One, Chapter 4

53 See Nietzsche's *Human, All Too Human: A Book for Free Spirits* (1878)

54 Adam Zagajewski: *A Defense of Ardor* (2004) pg. 8

55 Pre-Socratic philosopher (624-546 BC). Rejected mythology as an explanation for the natural world.

56 "Religion and the Artist: Introduction to a Poem on Dante" (1928)

57 Brown, Murphy, and Malony: *Whatever Happened to the Soul: Scientific and Theological Portraits of Human Nature* (1998) pg. 74

58 An oft cited, but most likely apocryphal, sentiment attributed to Pierre-Simon Laplace (1749-1827).

59 See the writings of Morris Berman, Chris Hedges, and the "New Atheist" movement

60 *Poems* (1895) From the Preface to the Third Edition (1901)

61 From *Fury* (2001) Chapter Seven pg. 87

62 See also the writings of Hermann Brock, Adam Zagajewski, and René Girard

63 See *The Age of Spiritual Machines: When Computers Exceed Human Intelligence* (2000) and *The Singularity is Near: When Humans Transcend Biology* (2006)

64 http://www.dailyscript.com/scripts/annie_hall.html

65 See Newton's Second Law of Thermodynamics

66 Anti-theists like Christopher Hitchens frequently employ this term in their writings and lectures. See *God is Not Great: How Religion Poisons Everything* (2007)

67 See the writings of Neil Postman

68 "Time to Pretend" from the album *Oracular Spectacular* (2007)

69 From "Preface to Richard Wagner" Trans. Shaun Whiteside

70 From "British Association Visit to the Abbey Theatre" (1908)

71 See *The Divine Comedy*: Purgatorio (Canto 27)

72 The use of "artifice" here is two-fold. It suggests *workmanship*. It also suggests *fakery* and raises the possibility that the entire vision is a dream.

73 From *Praising it New* (2008) "The Isolation of Modern Poetry" (1941) pg. 154

74 Ibid. pg. 154

75 See Stan Smith's *W.B. Yeats: A Critical Introduction* (1990) pg. 34

76 Ibid. pg. 34

77 Ibid. pg. 34

78 Marx: "A Contribution to the Critique of Hegel's Philosophy of Right" (1844)

79 *The Aeneid* (III, ln. 32-63)

80 Jennifer Medina: "Warning: The Literary Canon Could Make Students Squirm," *The New York Times* May 17, 2014 (Online)

81 Ibid.

82 See Orwell's *1984* (1949)

83 See Tennyson's "Ulysses" (1842) ln.18

84 See "Archaic Torso of Apollo" (1908) ln.13-14

85 Hobbes' *Leviathan* (1651) is instructive here.

86 See Hayek's *The Road to Serfdom* (1944 - 2007 reprint) pg. 77

87 *The Exhausted West*, Harvard Magazine (1978) pg. 22

88 See Plato's *Republic*, Book VIII

89 A rewording of Judges 21:25 and Proverbs 21:2

90 "On the Sublime" Trans. H.L. Havell (1890)

91 Ezekiel 12:20-25 (NRSV - Anglicized)

92 *Yeats: The Man and the Mask* (1948) pg. 6

93 *The Weight of Glory* (1942)

94 See Eliot's "The Waste Land" ln. 175

95 See Donne's "Holy Sonnet 10" ln. 8

96 *Nostalgia for the Absolute*: "Does Truth Have a Future?" (1974) pg. 50

97 See Pascal's *Pensées*: "The eternal silence of these infinite spaces fills me with dread." No. 201

98 See Hopkins' "Pied Beauty" (1877) ln. 1

99 See Melville's *Moby Dick*, Chapter 7

Made in the USA
San Bernardino, CA
08 March 2016